RESTLESS WHITE FIELDS

POEMS **BARBARA LANGHORST**

restless white fields

NeWest Press

LIBRARY AND ARCHIVES CANADA CATALOGUING IN PUBLICATION
Langhorst, Barbara, 1958–
Restless white fields / Barbara Langhorst.

Poems.
ISBN 978-1-897126-79-0

I. Title.

PS8623.A527R48 2012   C811'.6   C2011-906751-X

Editor for the Board: Doug Barbour
Cover and interior design: Natalie Olsen, Kisscut Design
Author photo: Valerie Koroluk

NeWest Press acknowledges the financial support of the Alberta Multimedia Development Fund and the Edmonton Arts Council for our publishing program. We further acknowledge the financial support of the Government of Canada through the Canada Book Fund (CBF) for our publishing activities. We acknowledge the support of the Canada Council for the Arts which last year invested $24.3 million in writing and publishing throughout Canada.

NEWEST PRESS
#201, 8540–109 Street
Edmonton, Alberta T6G 1E6
780.432.9427
www.newestpress.com

No bison were harmed in the making of this book.
printed and bound in Canada 1 2 3 4 5 13 12

for love

no
kind
words

CARE OF THE NECK

i thought i had done with hatred
and grief   my father's

insurgency   his painting   my peace
in his excellence still i cannot defend this

my mother is essence
such stalled mitochondrial chill of regret

each sleep   i share her cooling body
no wool no flannel no linen   can warm us

through watershed moments   motion sickness
or hubris   you're never so close

such a bullet of fears   love's anaesthetist cried
by her ear as she slept   all hope lost

the one clear way to raise the dead
may be to absolve the living

MAY TRIAGE

i

cutthroat cliché opaque french lilac moaning or leaven hearts greening
viridian brome grass infiltrates our beds quick columbine calling

hay turns to shit and to dust or we suffer the violence of breath
in broadest scale rhythms like lilacblue skirts in the sky of her leaving

french leaven moons bend to new hunter's green scat in my heart and to love
in each calling may blanching grass my deepest direction a blind desiccation o

heaven enduring slow gravel road lined with trailer park plaques in a room with
a viewing crewel seas of eternity beds lie in dust in hunter green calling

a loon spring a lake heart tossed now in flames a devil's herb darkling
blonde skull asplinter small bullet remarking the sky of her leaving

apricot rose o violent spring each lilac a blueing blindsiding may tracks
in my breast so black dog infested return in each cycle recall my despair

the weighting viridian fields toss deep sighs for lakes rising harmonica heart
dancing dust flames repulsing repairing the skirting each bluest spring view

ii

bonfire blast gasoline twist in my gut motorboat rush setting milk
flaming cartons afloat on the past syncopation the tune kindling a spring

played in july one room school house of fire works right through the grass
the garden dramatic digression of tangent and cosine and motors from wine

corks or moose call and duck whistling three-year-old dancing in days free of fear
feathers pluck hunting with camera so twisting the sixties in verse in a mind

rhyming targets his focus on honour too bold to end in stigmata precision 'he's
cleaning his guns' a workaday rush faulty translation so blind in his sights

striking common as milk devastation mixed media crashing wild indigo waves
in our brains horrid darkling our darlings a failure o faulty spring dance

boldly away leaving childhoods erased no sound in the pluck
of a rifle the twist of a shotgun roar such shattered syncopation

of moonlight sonata tight tide bursting blue rush gallstone hammers
return the repressed a bilious brightness twists and persists this mayday strike

iii

the green leaves unfurling fulsome and feral unceasing thoughtnoise
spring eye rises past brittle limbs shiver an endless resistance o keening

rebellion persephone's crimson seed bile-driven fury the gall of dark fat
days see earthly abundance suspended demeter deranged all life awry

murder abduction life   below suicide spasms irradiate   bladder
some faint release belladonna the devil's cherries illumination

the black dog barking at grounded geese flocking the fields
a white pause long lonely sky painted high and glowing

see the unseen alazarin fruit taste return the repressed
uncanny queen of the underworld turn me from iron

longing winters to april may june no warm melancholy
just naughty man's cherries no devil's herb healing

no nightshade reprieve
this pomegranate trick

MENSTRUAL CUP

•

time is a series
of infinitesimally small slices he tells me
though that number may in fact be finite
•

i have been blue forever azure cerulean indigo the most intense
aqua and ultramarine despite my fear of deep water
last night i poured my
garden into an envelope spattered paper with small black
worlds of blue weathered
delphinium pods
of coarse
gold silk sugared
and wrung into haute
couture

divine

the mathematics of fatigue
the colours of grief and release
•

for thirteen years i can't forgive

• • • •

to understand agony is violence itself
a good man a good mind holds an energy too dangerous to know
•

i am afraid to hold a knife

i cultivate tibetan blue poppies and choose paint chips
approximationsthingsstandingin
for

i am an escape artist

i can't even tell you
how i came to this conclusion

•

there are no kind words for this
my father put a bullet in her brain and a shotgun to his chest
•

the world is a temporary instability
booms brother kurt with
buoyant good humour

•

forty years ago
summer at the lake
bright blue waves crashing
my mother sees my father attempt
with much persistence and little success to hoist
the pea green boat atop the car
•

she shakes her head and says
he's a good man

the media made it door to door before the cops

•

twenty years ago stroke scrambled he says

some
of the things we never
compromise on

are the things we like to eat •

• compromise • no •

his wits return

but not his sense

•

•

twenty years ago
we find them three days later

•

at the wake a woman in carmine red
his first fiancée her shocked embrace
I could have been your mother

•

no

my mother would have said *if you don't laugh you'll go crazy*

•

wilson's bowl honours a man and a woman who never met while wilson ended his metaphysical
letters to lilo some time before he shot himself in his office his suicide
their relationship or the fact that she soon

walked into wild indigo waves forever

almost escapes his friends' tribute

the world is as sharp as a knife

•

pride in mind alone

•

stroke of genius strike
a pose
i transfix myself with
images
transformation
flirtation with infinity
the model's exquisite torture
curl of an octopus pinned atop a perfectly sculpted head

•

if her grey blue eyes are never named
if her now dead sister never cries

why are there no
tissue boxes in this church

if i never see her dead dead face

if a man and a woman never met

•

my son
is on call
seven times for
seven times five hours
in seven times four days
the stress without
end or beginning

barely
four percent
who reach
code blue

return

•

the world is a very narrow bridge *what is most important is*
not to be afraid

no, the whole universe is a thought/ *ruptured/ just short of*
completion . . .

•

no no know
kind words
spattered
•
•
can ease my

buoyant worlds
of blue weathered
instability a visitation

could she have walked into wild indigo waves of
•
•

guilt *manifold*

the colour of
complexity *reduced to a graphic*
singular surface *mark*
certain violence
no fixed value

•
•

my scraps of Christmas velveteen
r age
suicidalityachi
ngdesp
air

my daughter's menstrual cup
scarlet wounds of cyclic release

guilty love encircling

i dream in colour

i sleep
in my street clothes
•

.

waiting

.

a
ten
-yea
r
trans
for
ma
tion

not
a cur
e
but
a
cal
ling

.

ultramarine sweater indigo car
deep teal chairs phthalo floor cerulean cupboards
and at last

muenster
a monastery

the blue door

•

bellum

NOVEMBER AFTERNOON

tall flags of weeds
on the left side only   deepest umber
or dark sienna   so long since i knew
the mysteries of paint   in the foreground
the remnant of a rusted buggy
a thing i begged my husband not to bring
when we left quill lake   it stands
just before the pale tall grass
that surrounds a spotty line
of spruce emerging beside bare
lombardy poplars
as a windbreak
this is a seasonal
disaster   even in summer
the trees are barely decorative   and block
the view   in the background lies
a field of grey beige weeds   pockets
of dried grass and more dark spikes
half-circle of scrubby poplars
and willows   grid road   barley field
where once we found the neighbour's
cattle   the sky is blunt grey cotton

repeat throughout the landscape
with variation

MORNING

i

morning mourning morning   a grey day   woolly light layers cloud   llama sky
spitting rain weeds burned red and tall as saplings wave   shapely lombardy
poplars   frail long to retain composure but fail a field of canola across the grid
unset unsettled to be or not to be — cut — without the harvest

i sip
from my chipped cup   the red truck
exhausted

piles of *humboldt journals* huddle in corners of the room weeks-old news
stacked a mass of photos and bylines   guest of *the daily show* reports on *the*
world without us   twenty years to oblivion   a legacy of bronze and plastic

ii

piles of grey wool
light stacks of llama sky

weeks old weeds burned red
canola frail as frantic saplings

lombardies   unsettled composure
red truck without the harvest

flutter of plastic and *humboldt*
journals hoarding bylines

plastic oblivion
bronze remains

the world
without us

RESURRECTION

the mind says that you can see the spirit of the dead rise as perfect humans
in shades of blue or lilac as they flee

angel the ghost of your faint black apron over thin white shirt steps the still room
stands above me sad and shaded can't or won't bend or kiss just gaze
and raise the intimate self   the fractal catastrophe of human time
your steps corner the bed your living death fades forgotten in tissue paper slips

snow falling lyric may or april flakes pause suspended above the black ground
poised for grief to green with entanglements

CLIMATE CHANGE

my daughter
i am becoming
strange
i set aside
bones
broccoli stalks for soup

my newfound urge to conserve

a fridge full of rotting cucumbers in putrid sheaths
bags of fake baby carrots huddling upon the
lower shelves

two opened packages of browning radishes

lingering closer to my line of sight

plastic box of once-lovely

organic salad displays

the costly mummification
of my best intentions

my mother never
said much

about the

environment

it was she

who supervised

radiant as summers
at the lake

slow-handed, i gather loose
strands — / intimate /
grey traces of
a mind, fine pencil
lines, the letters of a name.

[not] another earth mother —

fireworks

the last day
the inevitable

soggy three-day
holiday week [the mosquitoes overwhelming
end — at her funeral]

nature — she was the interface — man-made danger
fold-up raincoat and thin plastic hat
permed blonde curls
smoking her cigarette
in public
lit each fuse

i found / a thing to do

i had to look up
that linebreak
my father's browning

late in his career, degas turned
to poetry

the poet as instrument [...]
the dancer not as a person but as a metaphor

life
a series of passions inscribed in our dying cells   write-
offs   precise imperfections

three days the bodies lay

clearwater ripples over history & faith
revolutionary acts & the words of our forebears

only the harsh intake of breath uh uh uh
the dreaming man remains

if i deny
synchronicity

how

I crave to give I carve to crave
I crave to hold the knife and carve myself

every three seconds how I have missed her
beyond marrow or shelter

contemplation a countermeasure to violence

steeped sixty years in dreams of escape

murder is murder is murder is murder
a shot in the dark   *three times her little throat around*

the stillness of the abbey
the pervasive quality of prayer

haunted by sublimation
i repress

demented i refuse
to undertake
anything

my mom taught me the front crawl,

the intermittent breathing,

the year we
forgot her birthday

the perfect deep breaths

new year's eve
for god's sake

in between strokes. but

my favourite was swimming
to the bottom and holding my
breath there as long as possible.

here one is given the music through the gesture

dear god, she thought. how easy death would be
if there was death and nothing more

yes

uncanny i pray for the return

the dead have always written to us
with their invisible ink.

every moon milky
fragile.
a tenuous life

then they deliver us

back to ourselves
in slow blooming

seasons

distance space

. . . . . .

what is it to move in

the
deceptions of a

world without a mother
to go on teaching of
time
the great
ocean beneath all that is said?

cranberry-red remnants atop bare 6 a.m.
hedge windless the ancient dog wills me outside
exhausted leaves drop like slow rain in the hint of a
fog

long ago kicked by a horse her old back breaks like new
I am forced to a ferocious love
have her sleep the last sleep

nine cups of coffee . . . cannot help but feel

my father's broken choice
cannot help but know that time between time

when she was shot and he was not

my mother's slipped-disc back
he would prevent her pain, his loss —
or so he

thought

my patient jewish friend reminds me of my one sane dream

my mother will come to me on rosh hashanah
for chinese food

all these years

and still

i am

starving

INSOMNIAC SUITE

iridescent
muse-
sliced nightmare

firstlight
snow-
fall

feather-
stitch pinch
opaque twitch

slip
fold blue eye
slight

TRANSLATION

wasted names
a tracery of what is
[invisible]
a phrase
a place
a plane
a planet
the illusory
the slip by lip
translation line by line buy
benjamin's tangent and cosine
mad perpendicular clarity
narrative preached in the original
sin

the persistence of memory

VIGILS

■

the things that want to be caught as they rush by are not meant
for anyone's ears
▪

isabella sent me
grained with gold...the only thing that has broken in

■▪

what we call the white   albumen   is clear until whipped or cooked or transformed
into skeleton   feathers   innards   the egg-white soul transparent silently builds
and feeds off the bold yellow body we view as our defining characteristic
▪

her bones were never found

i hold a shard of pottery the only remnant of the bowl my sister made me   it has all
the colours of the original   indigo and lucent mango grained with gold   the white clay
prominent at the edges completely irreplaceable the only thing broken in our move

■ she came at me before I could approach her
refused the barn
■▪

in the unorganized hamlet of burrows   our new home hosts a summer of apricot kittens
d'artagnan yorick and horatio   playing in the perfect blues of larkspur

daily occurrences mark a vigil
the terror or *the erebus*

■▪

▪ outside our world hamas captures six israeli soldiers and holds them
drawing tensions into war the israelis bomb lebanon and the lebanese retaliate with less
effect the israelis in fact do hit the un observers despite repeated messages about location

faulty translation

■ *i am quite sure she felt*
that i have reconstructed my knowing
completely irreplaceable the thing that has broken
our inability to discern ▪

■
we fall in love with a trio of sofas each called *bella* find that the lipizzaners
often name their stallions this too pop-television crime-lab show *isabella sent me* images
of dark paint horses proliferate for me these mark
a vigil the dark horse is calling for me or waiting

■
the error in faulty translation
repeated messages about the location
meant for anyone's ears

▪ horatio horatia is dead too cold to bury her the thigh bone her meat
torn away lies inside her open belly not repulsed by what i love i find her face
i am quite sure she felt no pain the bag does not reveal the lower jaw open in terror
and I choose not to uncover it I stroke her face above her
open eyes frozen
in surprise like my own

■ ▪ *things that want to be caught as they rush by are not meant*
we broke her in a week
she was beyond us   clear until whipped or cooked or transformed into
the skeleton
the white clay beneath
we should not be surprised

the hms terror or *the erebus*

■ bella tangles a hock in the barbed wire fence she stands puzzled   ears moving discerning the pain   she leaves me lunging to wrench the needle from her neck charges me the vet's words echoing *just don't get killed doing this*
▪

sixteen hands dark head and markings on white black mane and tail perfect blazing intelligence curious eager   so dangerous   she is beyond us   her new owner comes by to say *we broke her in a week*

■   i search her name and discover   what?

lies inside her open belly i am not repulsed

by what i love
moving discerning pain

horatio's death   six months to the hour of her birth   she has to be where she never hunts   a mile from home   to run under the wheels of my own husband's car as he leaves minutes early for a job he despises
■

repeated messages about her location
isabella sent me   some trick of timing ▪

spring   isabella's owner tells us that she did not come home after the first
blizzard

tangled discerning   beyond clay or crush

■

they know lieutenant john irving's bones by his medal for mathematics his father
my ancestor   warned him that all of his friends of influence having died
over the winter
john had best remain in the navy or emigrate to australia   he chose australia
▪

some trick of timing and promotion
set him on franklin's final expedition

the *hms terror* or *the erebus*
i can never remember which

open eyes   frozen in surprise like my own
it is too cold to bury

bold body grained with gold

■   the dark horse calling me   or waiting

easy to think that she needs us to find her   to touch her remains in the way that i
handled horatio's   but my knowing tells me that she is driving at me   a dark
thing all love
and terror
rising out of the impossible situation

▪■▪

i search her name and discover   *isabel* means *devoted to god*
bellum means *war*

WESTERN

this morning i knew wilderness at last woke from my grief
the earth writhing in the hands of my deepest fantasies

one blind sighted cliché to dream
hyphenated promises

            a system of indulgences
the garden the intrinsic cerulean
    of imagined symmetry
        castaway

luther in his very grave

every minute the man a civil word down the hall
implores demands help

me

bones awry beyond the *terror* fascination family intrigue fame and famine great
great uncle irving's mathematics medal marking pride a frozen plain a faulty
planned promotion sister ship to franklin's *erebus* such vesicular hubris
in the obsessive who would court his fate with vessels named for fright
and the site where men were neither dead
nor quick
the parade of steam a model manifest
three years' ration raisins suet pickles chocolate mustard pepper soap
thirtythreethousandtwohundredeightyninepounds of horror in lead-soldered tins

time stops

in the basement where my father types john irving's letters

near the coldroom where he will someday shoot himself

IN THE NAME OF THE FATHER

i slept better before you
learned to kill
anxiety that perfect cure
now i share szumigalski's
fear of knives i cannot stand to see
flustered chickens
popped in cones
heads thwacked off pre-cordon bleu
it takes so much rage
to learn
to love
to squeeze
a cupboard moth
immortal birds they fly at us
their suicide my potent fear
of being
god's *beetle*
in leonard cohen's hand
i slept better before you learned
to kill

SILENT SPRING TWO THOUSAND AND SEVEN

for terri brunet

the river bisects the highway on either side of our home we are stranded
in a house hoisted on pools of eyes silver duct-tape shimmer
frog song seeps in at the sills

the sealers are wedged in the ice off labrador but the press assures us no
worries they will hardly suffer the fate of great great granduncle john irving

boats are crushed helicopters unable to land the sealers become worried
peeved with the injustice the inexplicable failure of government
in the 21st century
to dominate the environment

privately drowning in her lungs aunt terri is battered by a swat team
of specialists who do not specialize in her disease she has had symptoms
for two years tested and dismissed as a crank
note missing from file in german *krank* means *sick*

as unbearable three weeks pass x-ray too late to biopsy she slips panicked
into what we pray is an unconscious state in restraints in the ICU
life support inflates her tissues
as her children in their outrage say she has become the *michelin man*

as she lies in a coma the hospital honours her on her birthday with balloons
wishing her a wonderful day the mortician abhors makeup and at the prayers
her daughter quietly beseeches each relative for a little red lipstick or blue eye
shadow
for her mother's dead face

LITTER

for loudon wainwright III

i

eye
bouncing on the washed out road
furred tennis ball bits of black and white
punctuate the gravel
two miles a-
part

the misery of skunks

ii

driving hard on highway 5 glancing side to side   dodging   a splatter of fox
a clump of feathers ungodly haste on the verge a stiff still full-grown raccoon
legs up   immaculate no sign of the kill a teddy bear of dead things —

iii

new growth found
up bush's ass

cheney   gardener appointee   where's the malathion

structure is fine   i prefer freefall
oh flee my mirror   it's adam smith

delphiniums plunge around the back door
a foliage of friendship

folks won't buy this climate change
temptation's truth   the devil is a beautiful man

too hot for breath   leaves fall into yellow in mid-july

crumbling roads crisscross the prairies
alberta paves its paths with gold . . . *black gold texas tea*

iv.

my father said they'd come for our water

sophocles said the keenest sorrow is to recognize ourselves
as the sole cause of our adversities

mulroney said nafta would benefit all parties

peas won't set   cats won't care
i am writing this poem *against despair*

BELOW THE WIRE

i

to gather the dead resurrect a flattened hawk i don't know when it started
a puff of down a beak an eye marking my path i have been for forty years a
prophet on the highway each car flicks to life some long thick umber wing flaps
and resettles for i am not revolted but afraid rueful wanting

to approach the place of holiness

ii

last autumn's fall expedition to the graveyard our chickadees went wild for my
students the romantics' dead thoughts chanting confusion all through the lane
of the yellowing elms this year's fashionistas their connected hundred-dollar
dresses become distraught with the cool west wind but they have dirt
on the mob as we sit beside the monks reading shelley's
ode to the unified wish for

a cold climactic change of heart

iii

mystics say that the bird flies in the calling a fully-fledged mark a catalogue i exchanged left by some trace of a past event or dead vultures the litter of holy cattle an interactive vestige of corpses or a crisis called humour in a million animatronic signs or a clue seeing the picture of god's sense of my agency the threshold to which I may aspire i find a fake parrot to be trained by plastic crackers to sleep when the lights fly and dim jokes crack on command and tell that there is no way to dispose of those that die

by the flames they build themselves

OBSESSIVE

a firehorse of pain
rides me   my
curried
eccentricity   reason's brittle
bridle slung too tightly

i feel it failing
worn thing

i catalogue
revulsion

cat's whiskers
spiny aspect   pokey reeds
thrust stiff through ice
talking spruce cones cluster
fearfilled feathers

they never tell you how
a mystic mind must pay

i hear bella calling
her shattered body

erupting femur splinters
entrails
frozen mane still spooling
flattened hawk's wing rising
gesticulating weather

my bright bright tree of knowledge
feels franklin's circumpolar storm-blast

EROS

eros i have eros in every single socket my x-rated disease is just a highrise of
bright cocktails my specialist distills with pride and light accomplishment you
never see my secret pain a stiff epistemology a department of biology will never
button up my frame my world i cannot bend it i will never be as i once planned
it time ensures that i am guilty of dead mice and many rats   but alive between
those hidden faulted points i feel quick ruptures of my sanity my radiant
disease gives my wild life to the plan that i am eros i am eros i am

STRANGE BIRDS

at the yukon delta goose chase sex it fold it band it slide each wildlife
biologist's avian neck beneath its wing shove a flu bird's swab up its cloaca
for should such flu be detected we will as a breed of syncopated snotheads
ensure the net corral of variation with tagged birds' breast feathers
to complete the prophecy the spread of the domesticated virus
to our motley incarceration
by the news brood flying massacre

ORBIT

this is not a poem to be captured in the moments before sleep   when
the past is just an ache

the
deadliness of
detail cresting after years of blight

the yin and yang of cats upon the table
marking eliot for god's sake
prelude to her pain

elizabeth's proliferative retinopathy
insanity of weak capillaries
sweet oath of god
crab apples burn and crack black
seer bound in blind
capillaries
popping insanity
orgasmic stress six hundred laser cuts a strobe a

strain   boil in boiled containers
boil and boil

SWIFT

shy containment or keening self-induced taciturnity   who can tell   he lies
silent inside outside doorways only   lets me stroke his black and white
body of cat-crossed limits all self-distraction punctuated
mapped in the compulsive plucking of hair   the worry of self   does he wrestle
with penance shouting things in greyscale   his threshold
bare lines of lonely waiting   i wonder what he was or will be
lesions of his other lives

GALL

there is such intimacy with the body in pain that one can come to crave
a pot of custard a trivial drop of pursuit a warm dish of tikka masala to ignite
the death projecting incarnation near pique that a lot of fat produces
an encounter with an ontological sensation in the gallbladder not dissimilar
to those who dare to hang themselves know that to increase orgasmic intensity
the irregularity of false love of success determines potency through the liquor
of settled stomach or the heat of bursting screaming breathless belly one comes
to feel the martyrs and their self-flagellation

exiled hearts

COLD

sad ash fires my bones   silent marrow
burns   the theory of blood   DNA DNR   not loveless
such stark searing   my cold words cry
anguish   necessity
massacre
the long look

my dry eyes fix
on you

OBLIGATORY CARNIVORE

benjamin's nike faces the storm of progress wings pinned in the disaster
of our tortured misinterpretation of free will by the dead feathered capitalist
cat gods facing the future not as apocalypse but as an endless supply
of carrion eviscerated carapace and wing confront me those trickster
forces of wind and felines resettle it daily whatever my path
i can't avoid stepping on angels

humour is the gift
of predators to minds bound
by philosophy

SPRING ROMANCE

i

i haven't forgotten you
i'm just ignoring you

a colleague asked would a .22 rifle kill a coyote?

i would think so i replied a .22 killed my mother

weather channel warnings
blasts of snow high winds zero visibility

the perfect violence of spring

ten thousand guests at the burrows resort
cyclone of snow geese nomadic acrobats

black scraps aloft
below restless white fields

i couldn't work i couldn't watch

i was dying a congestive heart

failure

the doctor said

it was the flu

ii

he gave me belladonna
for bloat

spasms of the chest so strong
i couldn't breathe   to weep

and it was only

april

iii

organization
is the key to memory

our subject will not bear organization

my sister and i have papers an inch deep on the table
often held down

by cats

iv

we play
with the possibility of

Engram:

a hypothetical change in neural tissue

postulated in order to account for
persistence of memory

-- called also memory trace

v

threshold: Psychol. *An alteration in certain cells of the brain*
or nervous system, assumed to result from
various
forms of excitation
and to provide the physiological
basis of memory:
also called engram

vi

may   blunt aphasia

cyclic swarm   intractable moments
tornadic flock of congested impulse

cruel conspiracy
the recalcitrant dead

wrap these things in dailiness

the words you hear when no one's speaking
the hearse you met upon the road

three times this week alone

the priest who wakes you now to say
he's praying for your dead

your brother in his gaol cell your brother
sheets tight sheetstightsheets against   his neck
in his gaol cell against
            his hisneck

vii

my father perspired for poetry

alfred noyes on the landing
laughing on his way to work
look for me by moonlight
   watch for me by moonlight
i'll come to thee by moonlight
   though hell should bar the way

my mother's two apricot roses
floated in an etched glass bowl

even after the disaster
cleanup crew had been there

after his stroke   as she slept
in their twin beds made as one

he came to her by moonlight

later wept   pulled pit sock off slipped his
toe into the trigger of a shotgun aimed

at his heart   in the one room with a
vinyl floor

for our ease

viii

oh some mellow morning when april is stirring
and shaking her sleepy wee alders awake

my father was a poet   i was raised on poetry — its rhythmic longing
the beat of my father's romantic heart   what he didn't consider was that
keats was consumed without wedding his beloved   the atheist shelley
had his dead heart pulled from the flames by fellow hedonist byron
who was driven from britain for immorality and yet chose to die an exile
fighting a war not his own

ecstatic litany of spectacle   sly decorum
perverted compassion

my father wrote his spring itinerary completely in the romantic vein
despite his best intentions   i have long since tried to suppress this yearly
synaptic sonnet   to no effect

april 30
my father's birthday
may
mother's day
may 22
their wedding anniversary
may 26
my failure to avert their murder-suicide

may 29
their bodies found
june 6
my brother's suicide   murder
june
father's day

frantic memory   exiled heart in flames
accumulated ash-blast portraits

i cannot recognize my children on the street or in the shops   i forget
my phone number   and   when i try to dial   some quirk of the universe
repeatedly directs the call to a group of psychologists   i go to the doctor
who asks me to count backwards from five   and declares me sane

ix

imagine the clear cracked mirror   blind my spastic
sodden heart consume bloat with intoxicating bitterness

bring me back across the threshold   i study walter benjamin's mystic
revelations to divine with coffee grounds   wake   and redeem the dead
how i long to finish simply   and at home
with my father's poem

i'll open my eyes in the first blush of morning
to hear the great northland awaking from sleep

each love is quilted to another   fresh death   how
can it grieve me so to remember my isabella
when the spring started i thought that my loves were
released   the haunting
over
the poem done

but o they inhabit me belladonna the only
ease to my bloated heart repressed miseries
recall the uncanny subliminal romance

darkling i listen   and for many a time
i have been half in love

x

easeful death
called him soft names

belladonna   the devil's cherries   deadly nightshade
devil's herb   naughty cherries   naughty man's cherries
beautiful lady   porn star

hallucinations or living dreams

in another life
women dosed themselves with belladonna
opened intoxicating eyes

projected the fantasy of inner sight

drive my dead thoughts over the universe

xi

beneath my bed i keep my mother's perfect crewel work   the last thing
my father saw before he shot her   i write at their table in my dining room
listening to the geese in the fields around me i keep his painting of the rich blues
and greens and browns of a spring lake facing me as i look into
the living room

where i can keep an eye on it

CASSANDRA

fields of mist skin clouds the texture of god
his love on the grass and the swamp

no life showing just pauses beneath the bright fullness obscurity
a thin sun sets in baroque country madness

here the colour of blue rinsed in crimson and saffron
the road just above the mist here only here on the track from my home

on the highway the coyote streams through east to west
this year's hawk rests flat in the sharp world

blue placenta

PROOF

if in a d   b and c are implicit
then a f h l o r z is an alphabet complete

a soul of a family is
an impenetrable patience

for all members
falling silent as frosted egrets

how like leaf hoppers and elephants

longing we hear with one foot lifted
left posed before the frantic patterns

our universe demands
on elephant time meditative

risk leaps through the invisible
rhythm carries us to resume our

zeugma where hearts are resewn

rosie is in love with latin
for i am *say only* am
the verb form implies the subject

ROMANTIC IN THE TWENTY-FIRST CENTURY

it wasn't the flu
the sad stones in my heart simply ran out of room

gathered my soul   their longtime companion

set off to the site of my bile
predictable screaming   heart-gouging spasms

i was never so happy
as when the throes held me

near death and yet so alive so vibrant with pain

no coincidence then that the liver the seat
of emotions   sent enzymes in rockets

release me release me release me

those doctors so tried   but left me a relic
of poets long dead   belladonna or morphine

some gravedigger's game
transmigration or transplant

bring back my pain

GRADE FIVE MAP: THE DIDACTIC HEART

retreat what can be said of our wars

count our protests how to calculate
numbers in coffins in peaceful demonstrations

the wild will advance / turning from chaos protesters are herded not by such
animal tracks on the grid / irresistible forces as wordsworth and marx in

our nearest hamlet so tiny a place / our blue heaven the astronaut jigging his jib

a bevy of archaeologists meet at the / nexus of the ridiculous and the profound
pioneer hotel to show pictures study / the way to see the earth is as a thumbnail

slides the geometry of our ancient circles / know that all that we have is now

old so diminished that the road marker / all but erased our climate

has been destroyed this week we watch / changes and now fear
last deer traipse through ancient elms / prophets of worlds gone

in our back yard reappear with the horses / alone but unfettered

mid-day in the pasture a tribe / bent on nibbling each root to the nub

our owls own the night / ask the hard questions, but none will stoop to

answer / say not who but whose

TRIPTYCH

unplanned delphiniums surround our home
those at the north end of the east flower bed   what layers —

say lairs —   pin prayers
of old women   or odd women who

grow around the porch and up over the deck   upon this
a fine line

stretching to within inches of our back door
i water them softly between the stalks so   the place
the perennial   inconceivable

site   array of shades and shadings blue   resurrection of grace
many flowerings

and violets mauve with hearts just   naïve as novice plantings
cunning as black as seduction   never dreaming the death of

each floral temptation
or ultramarine with white   a late evening   the harsh beauty

sky blues that fade   of autumn   tangles of stalks drying
from lavender   to rubbish
oh

that such wilderness exists in the tricks of our traumas so very
feral vibrant and present to us their
orange strobelight of pathos stutters on not quite untouchable
tomcat some symbol of wholeness beyond
languishes in a state of such longing the self-stricken sun
on our place of pain look at what rests try to love
windowsills thresholds demand entrance
crying to come in greet warmly but consider the cost

EVE RESISTING

i

a woman was not born to tend a garden

the garden happens and — gravitas — some

draw to it

elegiac dirt verminating
rhizomatic quackgrass
calling come to me

compose me

ii

bring me faintest blue delphinium all foaming eyes and sinspilled hearts
        simple hues that breed and recombine

            with one mind only
             to breach the highest lintel of recombinant green energy

            blackthroated blue
         warbling cries smother brush-driven aphasic

symphonies

iii

drape peonies their sodden hearts past
stilts

read daylilies and david austin roses
                    in tactile dishevelment

a vernal seduction of yarrow and tansy

certain sinistral wilderness

FIVE-WAY DISTRACTION

i keep
my back to the scenery
i know (that chaos is   poetry)   deception of
blowing elm leaves   slender blue beardtongue   crowding
        masses of sweet clover   alfalfa   (quickened) quackgrass
invasion   bed preening swallows
                              horses   (in last year's hay)
rather than   knee-high bluegrass
(concentrating)
(blue) the secret   cloudless   or cloud-glossing
                                        unforeseen funnels
      (temptation)
in all the right weather   (temptation)
              (temptation)
no
                    (temptation)

TAKE THE TEXT OF GABRIEL GARCIA MARQUEZ

his decrepit angel appearingunderfoot in all rooms
simultaneously   he secretly takes feathered strength

to flee the *fear and glory* that tie the *double*
hooks   next morning strangers call complaining
that our horses (which through my morning eyes

stand still penned in our three-acre wood)
are at the holy shrine of carmel   pilgrims
thirty miles from here   the afternoon brings

mystery   my in-laws' cat feasts furtively
upon the garbage in our half-ton
while safe at home eight hours away   my daughter

finds her ten-years-younger namesake
in england through the internet   i struggle to untie
my own bedevilled memory   my sister's forays into alchemy

duplicity that cruel muse for blackjack
win or lose   the same confusion

WOODSTOVE

i've always wanted a fine room   creamy white walls   aqua and apricot print
on twill covered slipper chairs   light streaming through overfull thin white
cotton window dressings   patina on metal ornaments   pale teal vases

yellow daylilies and blue rhododendrons   ivory carpets on aged maple floors
tasteful and immaculate beagle well under one chair   a white chased fireplace
with a broad mantel   candlesticks   a gentle rural landscape leaning above

i am addicted to such thoughts   exquisitely torn   more distracted by draperies
and pristine nesting than the blue throated warblers that graced my daughter's
chic sixties trailer birdhouse (a gift from her brother) chic birds for a chic home

i have three kinds of cathair on most surfaces   a couch covered in sunlight
the most durable fabric we could find after the sofa was sliced wide open by the
laughing black lab who guards our home from strange cats but not strange folk

not that i would change my choices   we can hardly restrain ourselves from
adopting a terrier or taking in barn cats   the economics of fashion are too rich
for our taste   time and a strange brutality are the cost of white we pray in olefin

does it matter that our new woodstove will cost enough to completely refurbish
our tiny dream house   or dress the yard with out-of-zone rhododendrons
endlessly i remind myself that love is at stake still   so hard in july to consider

that even our modest lifestyle is all distraction   how we ignore the crises in sudan
or somalia indigenous peoples everywhere   lives falling while grain or rice line
storehouses   we will know the cold of january

without oil or electricity   broken economies

EREBUS AND TERROR:
NO NEW SOUTH WALES

eiders turn   folded
stone cairns crusade of

metallic mathematics
in sight of the

blunt
manifest lead

lines
of provisions

covetous tubercular
bones pre-empt
archaeological
pretensions

pry riddles
wry pain

DECEMBER 31

my mother's birthday

words humble the world
its intricate proposition a set of problems
in constant play

i no longer believe that silence is death
the german word *schweigen*
means to hold your peace   to be quiet by choice

i'm bemused by the days when i could not be still
when i knew i would go mad
in a wordless world

how such ease frees me

i write not against the silence
but into it

ORACULAR

how deny
a crimson silt
to teeth untouched

white linen parched
snow stained blue
for want

a bit of blood-
less women wander
a world made half

the price of white
incessant ache
replaced

each cramp-checked
mind made strange
so draw such

oddity a season
taste revolution
in paint

submit resist
consume

the one true
predator

illumination

APOCRYPHA

dugout surface matelassé in white
mercuric water below a message longing for an ear
for a trace two doubles
hooked last fall a reading watson's fear
and glory early frost meltwater seepage
ice too thin for tinny cries aflailing
flaying later no hide to waste tractor hooks
retrieving bodies blue with time placenta rubber skin

this world unheard o wretched aural
membrane vertigo tinnitus *berkeley's dictum*
thrashing wheeling chorus

no one writes of horses outside the cariboo
ten began six remain
the dead stand ever in my mind

NOTES

Quotations are shown throughout the text in italics and listed here by poem and page in order of appearance:

MENSTRUAL CUP

13 Michael Langhorst.

16 Phyllis Webb, *Wilson's Bowl*.

17 Rabbi Nachman of Bratslav.

sylvia legris, "Nerve Endings, Remainders; Jagged White," *Nerve Squall*, 15.

18 manipulation of passage published by Justus Nieland and Scott Juengel, "Benjamin's Urgency" (review), *The New Centennial Review* 5.2 (Fall 2005): 197.

MORNING

24 *The Humboldt Journal*, weekly newspaper.
The Daily Show with Jon Stewart, late-night comedy news show.
Alan Weisman, *The World Without Us*.

CLIMATE CHANGE

28 tonja gunvaldsen klaassen, "A Visit," *Ör*, 26.

Robert Browning, "Porphyria's Lover."

Jessica Locheed, "'Degas the Sonneteer': Transcending Disciplinary Boundaries and Building a New Aesthetic," *Mosaic* 40.3 (Sept. 2007): 103.

Stéphane Mallarmé, qtd. in Rosemary Lloyd, transl. and qtd. in Locheed 108.

29 Douglas Barbour, "breath ghazal 35," *Breath Takes*.

Browning.

30 Shawna Lemay, *Shy*, 8.

Locheed 120, referring to Degas.

Sheila Watson, Two, Part 14, *The Double Hook*, 56.

31 Sue Goyette, (*the dead . . . seasons*) "Homage"; (*what is it to move . . . said*) "Issa," both from *Undone*, 83 & 86.

VIGILS

37 Walter Benjamin, "Some Reflections on Kafka," *Illuminations*, 143.

David Caruso as Horatio Caine, *CSI: Miami* television program.

Sir John Franklin's ships.

38 Browning.

IN THE NAME OF THE FATHER

43 Anne Szumigalski, *Fear of Knives: A Book of Fables.*

John Keats, "Ode to a Nightingale."

Leonard Cohen, "The Beetle," *Death of a Ladies' Man* (reprinted in *Stranger Music,* 233).

SILENT SPRING TWO THOUSAND AND SEVEN

44 the Michelin Man is its company's enormous balloon mascot, shaped like inflated white tires.

LITTER

46 the defining moment for *The Beverly Hillbillies,* television sitcom 1962–71.

47 Timothy Findley, *Not Wanted on the Voyage* (inscription)

SPRING ROMANCE

61 Michael Langhorst to dog.

64 Neuroscience Tutorial, http://www.columbia.edu/cu/psychology/courses/1010/mangels/neuro/neurotutorial.html.

67 Alfred Noyes, "The Highwayman."

68 my father.

70 Father.

John Keats, "Ode to a Nightingale."

71 Keats.

Percy Bysshe Shelley, "Ode to the West Wind."

TAKE THE TEXT OF GABRIEL GARCIA MARQUEZ

86 "A Very Old Man with Enormous Wings."

Sheila Watson, *The Double Hook.*

ORACULAR

90 paint chip, True Value Hardware.

APOCRYPHA

91 George Berkeley's theory of immaterialism.

ACKNOWLEDGEMENTS

A few of the poems have seen print elsewhere: "strange birds" and "gall" were published in *filling Station* (issue 46), and CV2 ran "apocrypha" (Fall 2009) and "grade five map: the didactic heart" (Winter 2009).

I'm honoured to include the following in this book:

Excerpt from *Ör*. Copyright © 2003 by Tonja Gunvaldsen Klaassen. Reprinted by permission of Brick Books.

Excerpt from "'Degas the Sonneteer': Transcending Disciplinary Boundaries and Building a New Aesthetic," *Mosaic* 40.3. Copyright © 2007 by Jessica Locheed. Reprinted by permission of *Mosaic: a journal for the interdisciplinary study of culture*.

Excerpt from *Breath Takes*. Copyright © 2001 by Douglas Barbour. Reprinted by permission of Wolsak and Wynn Publishers Ltd.

Excerpt from *Shy*. Copyright © 2004 by Shawna Lemay. Reprinted by permission of Radiant Geranium Press.

From *The Double Hook* by Sheila Watson © 1959. Copyright @ 1966 by McClelland & Stewart Ltd. New Canadian Library Edition @ 1989, 2008. Used with permission of McClelland & Stewart.

Excerpt from *Undone*. Copyright © 2004 by Sue Goyette. Reprinted by permission of Brick Books.

Excerpt from "Some Reflections on Kafka" from ILLUMINATIONS by Walter Benjamin, copyright © 1955 by Suhrkamp Verlag, Frankfurt a.M., English translation by Harry Zohn copyright © 1968 and renewed 1996 by Houghton Mifflin Harcourt Publishing Company, reprinted by permission of Houghton Mifflin Harcourt Publishing Company.

My great admiration and gratitude goes to the team at NeWest, with special thanks to Doug Barbour for his terrific support and fine editing, to Paul Matwychuk and Andrew Wilmot for their true expertise and generosity, and to Natalie Olsen for her inspired work on the design.

I owe an impossible debt to Dennis Cooley, Carol Gossner, Lorri Neilsen Glenn, Nora Gould, Hazel Kellner, Robert LeBlanc, Shawna Lemay, Karen Lee Lewis, and Seán Virgo, who each offered the finest encouragement and support anyone could ask for. Miracle of miracles, Robert Kroetsch read the manuscript and urged me to send it out, writing "the noise you hear in the distance is me jumping for joy" when it was accepted by NeWest. His death leaves not just writers but the world bereft.

Finally, many, many thanks to Elizabeth and Al and to family everywhere — and, most of all, to Michael, on whose unfailing sense of humour and patient love I rely.

Barbara Langhorst was born and educated in Edmonton, Alberta. She holds a Ph.D. in English from the University of Alberta and teaches at St. Peter's College, SK, where she has had the pleasure of meeting many of Canada's finest writers. She and her husband are empty nesters who share their acreage with several pets and the local wildlife. *Restless White Fields* is her first book of poetry.